COLOURS OF CHRIST

Patricia Newland began writing poetry in 2000. She has been an Anglican minister since 1980, first as a lay reader and later as deacon and priest. She compiled *A Tapestry of Daily Prayer* (Harper Collins 1990, Servant Publicatons, USA, 1993), which is a compendium of Christian prayers selected and adapted to be used as a daily prayer book. Her poems have been published in various collections and in her husband's book *Discover Butterflies in Britain* (WildGuides 2006).

The poems *Curtains of Promise, A Place of Peace,* and *At the Cross* were first published in *Even angels tread softly,* Mothers' Union, 2003. *Meeting Place* was first published in Camcophony, Cambridge U3A, 2004.

The author thanks John Drew, Frank and Thelma Fisher, Brenda Lealman and her husband, David, for reading and commenting on these poems. She is especially grateful to David for helping to bring this book to publication.

PATRICIA NEWLAND

COLOURS OF CHRIST

LAWNDEN *Books*

Published by LAWNDEN *Books*
Ickleton Lodge
Ickleton
Cambs
CB10 1SH

ISBN: 978-0-9561923-0-1

First published 2009

Printed in Great Britain

Praise the Lord all people!

Respond to God's call

Aspire to God's love

Invest in God's joy

Seek God in all your ways

Everyone praise the Lord!

CONTENTS

COLOURS OF CHRIST

The love of Christ is ruby,
Passionate and free,
Red as a velvet rose,
A tryst of love with me.

The love of Christ is sapphire,
Navy blue as the sea.
Waves billow on the surface,
Its peace lies deep in me.

The love of Christ is saffron,
Comforting and calm,
Accepting and forgiving
As evening's gentle balm.

The love of Christ is violet,
Sad as a widow's tears,
Thoughtful and remembering
Through passing of the years.

The love of Christ is indigo,
Hope glistening as a spark.
I see its light in mystery
And follow through the dark.

The love of Christ is amber,
A golden, burning fire
To cauterise my wounded heart
And crown my heart's desire.

The love of Christ is emerald,
Bursting, alive and green,
Green as the early morning grass,
Refreshed and shining clean.

CHRIST'S COMING

PRAYER

Jesus Christ
Eternal Love
Shepherd King
Universal Light
Saviour, Lord.

Come, O Christ,
Hope of the world,
Rescue me,
Inspire me,
Save my soul,
Transfuse my life.

CHRIST'S BIRTH

His birth was unexpected
though prophets had predicted
the coming of Messiah
in little Bethlehem.

Mary was his mother,
young and unassuming.
An angel had invited her
to nurture the child king.

Fearful, but questioning,
she trusted his integrity,
going into labour
to bear the Son of God.

Shepherds keeping watch,
heard the sound of angels,
hurried to the manger,
praised God for his birth.

THE MAGI'S RETURN

They journeyed convivially.
They returned silently, shaken
by what they had witnessed.
Shared vision had brought them
to their knees in reverent worship
of the infant King of Love.

Holding his gaze, they finally knew
why they had journeyed so long,
seeking one to give their treasures.
Such strange gifts for a baby –
not all of them appropriate.
This king had no need of gold.

They were silent as they contemplated
the beauty and horror of his future.
Theirs too had been changed.
Once a familiar way,
now a different place,
their guiding star had gone.

CHRIST'S GLORY

AT THE CROSS

earth meets heaven
pain meets bliss
sorrow meets joy
sin meets grace
fear meets faith
law meets love
absence meets presence
death becomes life.

THE WAY TO THE CROSS

A bystander's account

'Crucify him, crucify him,'
screamed the crowd.
Pilate washed his hands of him.
Jesus accepted his sentence, alone.

He shouldered his cross,
battered by taunting shouts,
'Save yourself?'
'Where's your God now?'

Women sobbed, wailed.
Jesus commanded them,
'Weep for yourselves
and your children.'

Hustled to The Place of the Skull,
hands grabbed and snatched at him,
hammered nails in hands and feet,
crowned him with thorns.

VIA DOLOROSA

Bent by the cross,
bowed by our sins,
stumbling and falling,
you struggled on.
Sorrow broke my heart
as I looked at you.

For one full second
our eyes sparked,
shocked my soul.
I now know
you died for love –
for love of me.

CRUCIFIXION

Jesus prays from the Cross

Father, where are you?
Father, can you hear me?
Our Father in heaven,
hallowed be your name,
your kingdom come.
May your kingdom come,
your will be done –
Is this your will, Father,
to abandon me?
Your will be done. Your will be done.
Give us this day our daily bread –
and a drink – please –
I'm thirsty, so thirsty.
Forgive me my sins –
Sin has overwhelmed me –
My God, my God,
why have you forsaken me?

As I forgive those who have hurt me –
I do forgive them, Father.
Father, forgive them,
they do not know what they do.
Father, lead us not into temptation,
but deliver us from evil.
Father, deliver me from evil,
deliver the world from evil.
Father, into your hands
I commit my spirit,
for yours is the kingdom,
the power and the glory,
for ever and ever.

JESUS IS PLACED IN THE TOMB

That's that, then.
He's gone.

We'd hoped for more – far, far more.
We'd hoped
    He was the cure for all our ills;
We'd hoped
    He'd change the world;
We'd hoped
    He was our way to eternal life.
Now it's over.

Whatever else you say about him,
    He was a good man.
    He didn't deserve to suffer
    A dreadful death.

ALIVE!

Alive,	like a million stars at night.
Alive,	like a seagull in full flight.
Alive,	like a lighthouse in gloom,
Alive,	like a daffodil in bloom.
Alive,	in surprise of meeting,
Alive,	in presence of greeting.
Alive,	in tears and laughter,
Alive,	here, now, hereafter.

Alive!

EASTER

Spring flower in bloom,
Christ has burst the tomb.
Christ is risen!

At Easter,
darkness is light,
sorrow is joy,
death is life.
Love is eternal.

Christ is risen!

TRUST

NOLI ME TANGERE

Mary was the first to see him –
'Rabonni, Rabonni, Teacher, Teacher!'
She began to cover his feet with kisses.
This time there was no ointment
save the salt of her tears.

'My Love, My Love,' she murmured.
'Do not hold on to me,' He said,
'I am not yet ascended to my Father,
my God and your God.
Go. Share the good news.'

DESCENDANTS OF JESUS

Without the bearer of the Word
the voice of Christ will not be heard.
Who will receive it, cherish it, nurture it?
Who will support it, savour it, share it?
Without the bearer of the Word,
the voice of Christ will not be heard.

SEED OF FAITH

Tiny seed of faith
sown in dark soil
of materialism,
of complacency.

Grow, grow little seed
out of strife,
burst into life.
Shoot, flower, fruit.

CALMING THE STORM

We are afraid.
Waves surround us,
batter our boat.
We huddle together,
cowering.

Water envelops us.
We try baling.
It's hopeless –
it's coming in fast.
We are drowning.

'Master, Master, we are perishing.'
He rebuked wind and waves
and they ceased.
There was calm.
'Where is your faith?'

THE WORD

The Word said.
We fled.
Christ bled.
He gives bread.
We are fed.
We fled.
Christ bled.
We are fed
With Christ's bread.
The Word said.
We fled.
Christ bled,
Gives bread.

OUT OF DARKNESS

Out of darkness, a prayer,
out of depths a groan, a moan,
a stutter, a mutter, a longing.
Slowly, it begins to glow,
to be companionable.
Out of darkness
a marvellous light.

OUR WORLD

Starved of food and education
by neglect, abuse,
our lack of love.

Trapped in poverty, disease,
unemployment, homelessness,
our fighting.

Choked by anger, jealousy,
selfishness, greed,
our addictions.

Imprisoned by rules, regulations,
fears, doubts,
our helplessness.

LORD, HAVE MERCY.

WORDS

Words –
There are no words
to convey what I wish to say -
horror, anguish, loss.
I can't make it right
with right words.
I am lost for words
where rightness now
may never be.

LORD, HAVE MERCY.

MEETING PLACE

As the river rushes, races to the sea,
I'm in the shallows gathering strength
like a salmon, to leap against the flow.
Leap, leap, leap to a place of meeting!
Can I fling myself against this tumult?
Intention compels me to do the impossible
leap, leap, leap to a place of meeting!

PRESENCE

I did not have the sense before -
pre-sense to sense your presence;
nor inner sight to see within;
nor hearing for heart's music;
nor smell - delectable, as Julian wrote.
The Psalmist sang, 'O taste and see' -
God, let me sense your presence.

RELEASE

Release me, Lord, from my captivity.
Grounded, immobile,
I want to fly –
fly like a bird
soaring and gliding
in the power of your Spirit.

EVENSONG

Strewn like Sunday papers
along the pews,
we peruse our prayers
in desultory manner.
Our voices mumble and rumble
like passing cars.
O Lord, open thou our lips
and our mouth shall shew forth thy praise.
Trees wave off last leaves of Autumn,
Lord, now lettest thou thy servant
depart in peace, according to thy word.
We are unprepared
when a shaft of light
pierces our dullness;
the dust is dancing!

CURTAINS OF PROMISE

Open curtains of promise,
let in light.
Look for dawn,
the sun rising.

Open curtains of promise,
let in light.
Search for new growth
in your own life.

TRANSFIGURATION

I saw Jesus in a different light,
his clothes were shining white.
Near him Moses and Elijah stood,
'Lord, it is very good.'

When Peter spoke, a cloud appeared,
shrouding us in awesome fear.
Then a voice, 'This is my Son.
Hear him. He is my Chosen One.'

As this vision vanished,
I'm challenged on my way,
descend the mountain path,
communicate this day.

EMPTY CHURCH

This church is full of memories
of people now long gone.
Their spirit is alive today,
their prayers linger on.

ABSENT GOD

O precious Absence,
longing fills my soul
as I yearn for you -
Absence -
more present
than anyone else.

BUTTERFLY BLUES

Grubbing in the scrub,
foraging for food,
munching, crunching,
I've got butterfly blues!

Now's the time to stop,
rest on my resources,
inhabit my cocoon,
I've got butterfly blues!

Waiting for new life,
waiting for release,
waiting to take wing,
I've got butterfly blues!

LIFE IN THE SPIRIT

CHAPEL

O God,
build a chapel in my heart,
grace it with your presence.
Let me be guided by your light,
share in carrying your cross,
become a place of Resurrection.

THE COMING OF CHRIST

You who know your heart's intent,
will wait for him in silence –
for Jesus, our Saviour,
to come today.

FOR THE HEALING OF THE NATIONS

The leaves of the tree were for the healing of the nations
Revelation 22 : 2

New leaf from bud emerged
furled, curled, crumpled,
opening to light and life.

New leaf promises green
emeralds, dancing future,
nodding, waving, greeting.

Then cold creeps in.
Its cheeks redden,
chap, brown, dry.

Leaf wrinkles, detaches,
is swept up, crushed, mulched
for succeeding generations.

SUNFLOWER

Sunflower seed sown.
Eagerly anticipating life,
every day she looked
for signs of a shoot.

Sunflower, tall and strong,
full of leaf, bursts into bloom,
turns her face to the sun,
opens her heart to warmth.

Sunflower, shocked
by wind and weather,
lost her looks, shrivelled up,
became an oil of nourishment.

HORIZON

I keep my mind on a distant horizon,
reached from within
by daily steps in faith,
listen for the inner voice
that speaks of love to be trusted.

I keep my mind on a distant horizon
reached from without
by daily steps of compassion
to meet, speak, feel
the pulse of another's heart.

WHERE THE FOUNTAIN SINGS

I leave the procession
to enter my secret garden.
Clanging the gate behind me,
I push through brambles,
step over tripping stones,
wind down the pathway,
skirt the scented area,
turn right into the clearing.
This is where the fountain sings.

PEACE

Arched, silent and empty,
yet full of grace –
this place not beautiful,
but prayed in –
rests in my heart.

Let go tension
        stress
            worry
                fear.
Let peace descend lightly.

Peace speaks to the depths
in silence beyond words.
It satisfies mind, heart,
resurrects my soul.

WHEN CHRIST COMES

Looking, I do not see.
Listening, I do not hear.
Waiting, I almost give up.

Then Christ arrives -
overwhelming surprise,
though he's familiar
as my neighbour.

When Christ comes -
a personal encounter.
I am transfused
when Christ comes.

SUN AND STARS

At last the sun is out! –
promised for a long time –
day after day, mountain tops
were shrouded in mist.

At last the sun is out!
A new day is here!
The sun has burst through –
spreads growth, happiness . . .

At last the sun is out!
The world is shining new!
Joy! Joy! Joy!

At night, I see a million stars
surrounding earth's dome
like myriads of people, diamonds
sparkling, inviting my presence.

RESURRECTION

O Lord,
Your arms have cradled me from birth –
You suckled me, nurtured me,
taught me, guided me,
let me go upon my way.

O Lord,
I left you, departed from you,
made my own way,
independent, successful,
self-confident, dependable,
or so I thought, until

O Lord,
my world came crashing down,
my body let me down,
my self-confidence let me down,
my spirit let me down, down,
down to the depths, where

O Lord,
I found you waiting,
watching, seeking, longing
to welcome, embrace,
take me home.

MY LOVE DID GIVE ME CHERRIES

My Love did give me cherries
succulent and sweet,
and I did eat.

My Love did give me cherries
rounded and red,
and I was fed.

I tossed my stones down at his feet
in fertile ground
and I soon found

new trees sprang up
with blossoms fair
and fruit more rare.

My Love did give me cherries
succulent and sweet,
and I did eat.

KINDNESS INCOMPREHENSIBLE

O God,
centre of my circle,
circumference of my soul,
smallest intimacy, widest wilderness.

O God,
my both and, either or,
my less, my more, my little, my much,
within, without, wherever.

O God,
my when, then, now, how,
question, answer, instant, eternity,
something, nothing, everything.

O God,
my inner light in outer darkness,
my sky blue in blackest night,
You are kindness incomprehensible.

TRIUNE GOD

Holy is our God who made us,
who loves us as parent,
who watches over us,
cradles us in his arms.

Holy is our God, our Lord Jesus Christ,
who came to save us,
to rescue us, show us the way,
give us his life.

Holy is our God, Spirit of God,
who awaits our invitation
to accompany us, to be
our hope, joy, love.

Holy, holy, holy is our God,
whose love we know
in Father, Son and Holy Spirit,
one God, now and always.

EASTER FLOWERING

You who dare, look closer,
shudder that there was no room
for Christ to live on earth.
Do not stay with pain.
Look beyond suffering,
wonder at your gain.

Look again and see
his drops of sweat like dew,
his blood camellia red.
Our Lord of Harvest,
risen from the dead,
awaits you in his garden.

PRAYER

O God,
I long,
I hope,
I breathe.
I have no words,
O Thou, my God.
O Thou, my God,
I have no words,
I breathe,
I hope,
I long,
O God.

PRESENT TO THE MOMENT

Je suis,
I am, when
I remember
Just to be
Present to the moment.
Present to the moment,
Just to be,
I remember
I am, when
Jesu is.

THE HANDS OF CHRIST

Wave

Appeal

Outstretch

Touch

Heal

Bless

ALPHABET OF PRAISE

O Christ,
We adore you,
We bless you.
You care for us.
You are dedicated to us
From eternity to eternity.
Forgive us our sins.
Give us grace
To follow you.
May your Holy Spirit
Ignite us with joy,
Keep us in your love.
Lord Jesus,
Mystery is hidden and revealed in your birth, death, resurrection.
Nurture my faith, open my spirit to your presence.
Give peace in my heart.
Quieten my mind.
Restore my longing,
Save my soul.
Help me to trust you.
Unite us
In your love
For all people.
Give us victory
Over our divisions,
For the world's sake.
Your cross our inspiration.
O Lord, I yearn for you.
May zeal for your house consume me.

POSTSCRIPT

Colours of Christ, the title of this book, is an important concept for me.   Each of the rainbow colours manifests a different aspect of Christ's love. We may only ever be able to see one colour of God at a time, but all are present in Christ's love.

Where did these poems come from? I began writing in 2000, at the start of the new millennium. My first poem was *My Love did give me cherries.* I woke one morning with those words in my head. Other words or scenes have also just come. More often, poems have started as a picture or an idea on which I have had to work to put into words. These poems portray dark moods as well as joy.

Because we are so familiar with the four gospels, the sections *Christ's coming* and *Christ's glory* were the hardest to write. We know that Jesus called out to his Heavenly Father on the Cross. We know too that the only prayer in words that Jesus taught his disciples was the Lord's Prayer. It seems possible that he might well have said this prayer on the Cross as a source of strength. *Crucifixion* is written as a mantra from the Cross.

The section *Trust* may seem more like *Doubt.* In facing our doubts, we may be strengthened into a position of trust, as the apostle Thomas was. I have found trust in God to be a series of steps. We need to work through our doubts in order to move to the next step, when probably we will soon again come to another step. The disciples were tested and we are tested.

The 14th century contemplative nun, Julian of Norwich, has been an important influence on me. Julian had sixteen visions of Christ on the Cross. After twenty years meditating on these, she wrote *Revelations of Divine Love.* My poem *Presence* draws on her insight that God may reveal himself through all the senses.

Life in the Spirit is a continuation of the section on *Trust,* but looks forward to *Resurrection,* a new and eternal life in Christ. The *Alphabet of Praise* is my mantra, which reminds me of the varied and deep love Christ has for each one of us.

Patricia Newland